Beauty Fee Sabililah

By Lina Ahmed

Beauty Fee Sabililah

Disclaimer: The advice contained in this book may not be suitable in every situation. Therefore if in doubt or in a need of professional help, it is recommended that advice should be sought from a qualified medical professional or a licensed counselor, Any action that is taken as a result of the advice or strategies in this book will be done at the readers own risk and the author is not responsible for any harm. The facts in this book are compiled to the best of my knowledge. I am not an Islamic scholar, Therefore I apologize and ask for your forgiveness if I have made any errors. Throughout the book, the Prophet Muhammad (s.a.w) is mentioned and I have omitted using the (s.a.w.) after every mention of his (s.a.w) name. Please invoke salawat on his (s.a.w) name every time there is a mention. Lastly, the hadiths are collected from the hadith books that are published by Darrussalam, please find more information in the acknowledgements.

ISBN: 978-0-9958080-0-3

Layout by Penoaks Publishing, http://penoaks.com

Dedication

The Messenger of God stated that "actions are according to intentions and everyone will get what was intended," therefore I write this work in dedication to my Lord, Who has shown me through His Book, His Prophet and His Miracles what beauty looks and more importantly feels like. It is my hope that by His Permission, this work will aid readers in the process of understanding what it truly means to *be* beautiful. The ability to uplift, dream and transform are the mere fruits of a tree with beautiful deeply rooted stems. Similarly, the production of outer beauty is an auxiliary manifestation of our inner wellbeing. Beauty is the bedrock in which self worth and self-love find their home. And what ultimately begins on the inside will naturally illuminate into our world. With that, let us rise to a new understanding, a new vision and a new plateau of beauty.

Contents

Preface

Bismillahi Rahmanir Raheem

We begin in the name of God, praising Him, extoling Him, seeking His Help, His Guidance, His Love and His Beauty.

And as we ask our Lord for beauty, we recognize the centrality of beauty in our lives. That all good is essentially beautiful. We all want to *be* beautiful. To possess beauty, to behold beauty, to be surrounded and engulfed in it. Beauty is a multilayered, controversial and often contested idea. Beauty means different things to people. The notion has also changed throughout the years, so much so that what was considered beautiful in the past might not be in contemporary times and vice versa. Beauty occupies spaces in the physical, emotional and mental realms. It can be found in spoken and written word and as beings with sensing organs, beauty can be felt in a variety of ways.

With the advent of globalization and the spread of communication devices, we are constantly exposed to images, products and beliefs about beauty ideals that are usually conformist, exclusionist and elitist.

Above all they are empty.

Moreover, this socialization has materialized in a socio-spatial sense with the creation of shopping malls which are in part produced by the widespread decadence and mindless consumerism incited through advertisements.

As confined spaces, shopping malls espouse certain ideologies and practices that galvanize people around hegemonic understandings of beauty. The socialization within these spaces produce conformist behaviors and beliefs that overwhelm and distract us away from imagining different forms of beauty.

Malls are filled with numerous amounts of stores that specialize in a dizzying array of different cremes, powders and serums that promise to enhance beauty. As we exchange our money for these products, we quite literally buy into these promises under the presumption that beauty is purchasable and available to people with money. That somehow attaining beauty is as easy as smearing on lipstick and wearing expensive clothing. The truth of the matter is, that many of us are living someone else's fantasy about us. We are trying to conform to beauty standards that we have not set for ourselves. What are we trying to prove when we bleach our skin or contour our noses? And to whom?

These hegemonic beauty ideals that are continuously perpetrated by popular culture were created for you to fit into someone else's perception of beauty. The commodification of beauty is what we measure ourselves and others against. Therefore we only see beauty in binaries, either you fit the description or you don't.

We are the first victims of this oligarchical understanding of beauty, as we change ourselves to be of service to others.

They say that our hair is the wrong texture. Our faces are too round, our lips are small, our noses are too big, our eyebrows are too thin.

We have trapped ourselves in a reductionist understanding of beauty because of the psychological dismemberment of our bodies into parts. This dismemberment results in the commodification of body enhancements that we purchase in hopes of clumsily stitching together a new embodied being. One with a different nose, new hair, new eye colour, new teeth, new skin colour and the list goes on.

Is this beauty? Is beauty a bottomless, never ending pit that is chased when we are young and then something we try to grip onto when we get old?

When one's sense of self is constantly assaulted by dominating beauty ideals in social media and popular culture, this results in damaged self esteem in women young and old. Like rust on steel, this slowly eats away at our ability to *see* ourselves in actuality, unflinchingly stare at our unique faces and bodies without picking at ourselves.

More devastating, however is while we scramble to meet the litmus test of these beauty ideals, in the process we lose the ability to *vision* ourselves differently. Sight and vision are different aspects that are affected by the thought patterns and beliefs we harbor. Sight looks at things the way they are, for what they are; therefore it is situated in the present moment. Vision is in the future and it is couched in aspirations, dreams, hopes and values.

If we are to ever challenge these distorted narratives we need to move in the direction of an understanding of beauty that is different and not only reactionary to the dominate ideals. Because in many instances, reactionary resistance is primarily about the other person or another's ideology. So many times people are always caught up in resisting they don't realize that they are still focusing on hegemonic beauty ideals and articulating interpretations of beauty that solely rest in opposition to these dominate narratives. Do you think that abstaining from removing armpit hair is a reactionary idea of liberation or an organic understanding? We have to ask these questions to move in the direction of liberation because the most meaningful understandings of beauty are those that are built from within not solely in reaction to dominate beauty interpretations.

So What does Beauty Mean to You?

While there is nothing wrong with adorning ourselves so long as it is in accordance with the Islamic teachings, we need to wrestle with the question of adornment as the be all and end all of beauty. Is beauty that focuses exclusively on the outside while neglecting our inner well being healthy?

The truth of the matter is our skin will one day sag and wrinkles will etch our faces, but it is another type of beauty that will continue to carry us on through our old age and after we pass away. Similar to an acorn growing into an oak tree, this beauty is cultivated in our lives and its manifestations are so far reaching that they continue into our after lives. Therefore our beauty can enjoy immortality, if we tend to it.

This type of unyielding and self-generating beauty is embedded in the – Quran and the Prophetic traditions. You are probably thinking 'how can the – Quran and the Prophetic traditions teach me how to achieve a natural glow?' Allah has revealed many beauty secrets in His Holy Book as well as through the life of His Nobel Messenger (s.a.w.) However unlike mainstream beauty practices that focus only on the outward appearances, this beauty places inner wellbeing at the core, working its way up to embellishing the outer appearance.

When we look at the extraordinary creations of the stars, moon, rivers and animals we are essentially experiencing the plethora of ways that beauty can manifest itself. The way that the merging colours of a sunset bleed together to produce a mosaic in the sky, or the subtle twinkle of the stars against the black tapestry of the dark night serve to illustrate the various forms of beauty that exists. These are not the same types of beauty and they shine under different circumstances in different ways. It is in the night that we appreciate the luminosity of the moon and the shimmer of the stars. Whereas it is under the presence of the sun, that we are able to behold the vibrancy of colours that flame the sky during a sunset.

However as beautiful as these creations are, they all serve a purpose that transcends beyond their appearances. For example, in the Quran we are commanded to survey the flawless creation of sky,

"You do not see in the creation of the Most Merciful any inconsistency. So return (your) vision (to the sky); do you see any breaks?" – Quran 67:3

Although, our Lord describes its perfection in the aesthetic sense, the sky also serves a function beyond its visual beauty

"Do you not see that Allah sends down rain from the sky and makes it flow as springs [and rivers] in the earth; then He produces thereby crops of varying colors…" – Quran 39:21

The sky is a medium that is used to send water to the earth, which sustains life for humans, animals and plants.

We appreciate the sky on an aesthetic basis, not realizing that its function is beautiful, it produces beauty and its very being is beautiful. It is beautiful. As we are enamored with its colours, we often times do not connect that it is this same sky that sends snow, rain, clouds and acts us a buffer against the sun. Many of us viscerally appreciate the sky and usually do not comprehend the substance of its work.

It beautifies itself and others through its actions. Thus from the sky, we learn that Beauty is not a *state*, it is a practice.

Practicing beauty, is not as easy as adorning our appearances rather inner beauty manifests itself in our thoughts, opinions, judgments, speech and conduct.

Like the sky, our essence should be beautiful in that we are so internally filled with beauty that what seeps through us beautifies our outer world.

When the sky emits acid rain, the damage to the plants, soil and aquatic life come as a result of this action. Similarly, we must critically examine the maladaptive practices and thought patters that beget ugliness in our lives if we are to arrive at a different place.

It is only then, that we will experience beauty that is made by and for ourselves.

Contemplation

"I saw the Messenger of Allah, (s.a.w) on a brightly moonlit night wearing a red garment.
Then I started looking at him and at the moon.
And to me...
he was more beautiful than the moon."
[Tirmidhi]

We have heard numerous accounts detailing the physical descriptions of the Prophet (s.a.w.) as told by his companions and relatives.

Everything from his skin, his hair, eyes, teeth, mouth, his body and scent radiated beauty.

Physically, the Noble Messenger was well proportioned and aesthetically pleasing. He was of the most handsome of men yet his beauty had another element to it and was almost ethereal at times.

"Al-Bara' was asked, "Was the face of the Prophet (as bright) as a sword?" He said, "No, but (as bright) as a moon." (Bukhari)

Many times in life, we come across people who are beautiful in the physical sense, but when we engage in conversation with them, we find that the beauty that emanates from them merely exists on the surface. Theirs is a beauty that does not radiate from within. Their beauty is comparable to the shadow of a human instead of the true physical form. Shadows lack substance, weight and dimension and are only apparent under the presence of the sun. Similarly, beauty narratives that are reduced to visual perceptions limit our understanding of beauty, when in fact true beauty is to be felt with all senses.

The Islamic tradition highlights the symbiotic relationship between the Prophet's inner and outer aura. His beauty was not merely a shadow, rather his inner well-being made his beauty an *experience.* In that when you marveled at his physical form, you were only scratching the surface.

The Prophet's beauty was not confided to the physical boundaries of his body, rather his inner beauty was compared to *a swift wind.(*Bukhari) We *feel* the wind against our hair, we *see* the wind driving the clouds and we *hear* the whispers of the leaves rustling as our senses are simultaneously awoken to the different manifestations of the wind's presence. Therefore, beauty is to be seen, tasted, smelled, heard and felt.

Like the wind, the Prophet's beauty was experienced on different levels.

Allah the All Mighty, affirms and encapsulates the inner beauty of the Prophet in the Holy Quran:

"And indeed, you are of a great moral character." – Quran 68:4

It is interesting to note that Allah highlighted the Prophet's inner beauty by pointing out his character.

Because what made the Prophet beloved to Allah was his inner well-being. It is because of his character that he is continuously remembered throughout the years by billions of people.

And he only lived for 63 years. Yet his inner beauty has achieved a perpetual immortality. The likes of which we will see in full bloom in the after life.

Where is a beauty that is timeless and transformative? Where can we find a beauty product that will make us glow like the moon on a dark night? What makeup artist can give us a deathless beauty long after we are gone?

The truth of the matter is, the luminosity of his face could not be purchased at the beauty stores and neither can ours.

Internally, the Prophet maintained a balance of his desires, appetites and thoughts. This mental homeostasis was projected unto the ways in which he slept, spoke, ate and walked. Mental, spiritual and emotional states materialize into actions and words that guide our lives and form the basis of our interactions and relationships. The Quran teaches us how to love, how to hope, how to trust, how to eat, to spend, to talk, how to dream and how to live. Allah teaches us how to exercise beauty in all areas of our lives and when we implement these teachings we are beautifying ourselves. All praises due to the Most Beautiful, Who has left us both a scriptural and embodied guide on how to construct beauty.

"There has certainly been for you in the Messenger of Allah an excellent pattern for anyone whose hope is in Allah and the Last Day and [who] remembers Allah often." – Quran 33:21

It is by following the Prophetic example, that beauty is clothed in intellect, speech and conduct. We also learn that when beauty is cultivated, it looks like the person in the mirror and not some unfamiliar person in the glossy magazines or in cinematic images.

Despite all of this, many of us are continuously engrossed in cultivating beauty through acquisition, believing that our imperfections exist on the outer and not in our souls and minds.

We usually do not address the root causes of our inner shortcomings and neglect our spiritual wellbeing. While we focus on our lips, faces, bodies and hair, we should equally focus on our minds, hearts and souls. These are the tools in which we enter a space where beauty becomes an experience instead of just a visual presentation. Using our minds we can elevate ourselves from the pernicious habits and behaviors that keep us anchored in our ugliness.

Allah encourages us to exercise *Tadabbur* which means contemplating and reflecting over the meaning of situations and events in relation to God's teachings. By engaging in *Tadabbur,* we can begin to produce a beauty that is not dependent on external products in order to grow. Rather the nourishment for this beauty is found in critical self-examination built on the foundation of self-love. I say self-love because to love yourself, you must first begin to know yourself.

In order to clean ourselves we have to notice the dirt. Similarly self-improvement requires awareness of one's weaknesses, desires, needs and strengths. When we stand before a mirror, it presents our flaws to us plainly and unapologetically. However it does so without the unsolicited advice or insults. Rather it *shows us* with empirical evidence things that we have missed or overlooked, reminding us that we have work to do. It does not give us the solutions just awareness.

And it is with this awareness that we can work out the kinks and smooth the wrinkles in our blouses and headscarves. Self-examination shines a flashlight on how and why our self-esteem fluctuates when we are exposed to certain visuals or ideas. It is well known, that in numerous reality television shows, the main themes orbit around images of materialism, opulence and surgically augmented beauty. While we spend hours consuming these images, we slowly chip away at our own self-esteem and when this happens we spend inordinate amounts of money on various products, dieting practices and even surgical procedures. The truth of the mater is that you are moving towards the images you see and beauty is affected with what *you* put inside yourself.

Self-awareness would involve questioning the reason behind our purchases or dieting. Is it coming from a place of self-love, or self-doubt? Many times, when people feel small, they try to over compensate in ostentatious and aggressive manners. We see that they mask their insecurities with narcissistic or gaudy behavior because of the emptiness they feel within them. More times than not, there is no acknowledgment of the root causes of our emptiness or lack of self-esteem. To know is to be empowered. When we purchase, eat, watch, speak, and act what is the motivation behind our actions? Are we doing it because of external stimuli or internal self-doubt? Maybe both?

The Quran speaks about a man who was given wealth, however this gift did not transform into a source of freedom. Rather *"he entered his garden while he was unjust to himself. He said, "I do not think that this will perish – ever." – Quran 18:35*

How many of us are slaves to ourselves? To our appetites, to material objects, to our perceptions? To our delusions of grandiosity or to our feelings of inadequacy?

Allah teaches us that this man was not free despite the wealth.

He altered his mental position in relation to his Lord. He was oppressed because he forgot who he was. Oppression came with the change of mental state. The man did not use the wealth in a way that stimulated a heightened self-awareness. The challenge here was how do I negotiate this wealth with my identity as a slave of God. How must we use health, wealth and time to strengthen our weaknesses rather than aggravate them?

So many times we think that, we need these tools to be self-empowered or to feel whole. However power is not to be found in material objects. Rather, wealth, time and health are tools that we merely *materialize* our existing self-power. Not generate power. The production comes from within. These aspects are mere tools in which our power is manifested.

One of the ways in which one's character can be tested is by giving him wealth.

If the wealth turns him into an arrogant and superfluous spender, then he did not move in the direction of power rather it illustrated how he was already disempowered within himself.

The wealth was merely a flashlight that exposed internal pollution. Our choices in using wealth, time and health are only reflections of our internal health or lack thereof.

If we use wealth in a way that is wise, moderate and conducive to our spiritual development and well being, it becomes a tool for exercising our power and practicing beauty. In order for this to happen requires knowledge.

To know yourself is power. It is freedom. Freedom in knowing what you are enslaved to, what is poisonous to your soul to what makes you sad or even suicidal.

In the Quran, the word *taqwa* is used to describe people who are successful because of their vigilance over themselves, their thoughts and actions. To protect ones sense of self mentally, spiritually, emotionally and physically requires self-awareness and maintaining a *consciousness* in our daily situations. When we have *taqwa* we look at things through realistic perception, things are as they are. For example, when buying a blouse, being present within ourselves, would mean that we probe the motives behind our desire to purchase clothing. Will this blouse heighten my compulsivity to spend and re-live spasms of short lived happiness or will it be used for utility purposes? Even our choice of preference of one blouse over another that is less expensive would require us to be present. This is because many people choose to buy certain items over others only because of the appearance and even sacrificing the utility of the product at the expense of its appearance.

Maintaining consciousness would also entail that one recognizes that this blouse is just a piece of material that will not fill me. Being present would mean that we would look at our state of mind before and after the purchase and examine if we felt a rush of happiness after we bought the blouse because we felt that we needed materialism to give us *permission* to feel whole. Having *taqwa* would question these feelings of misplaced self worth. In a state of *taqwa*, we would strive to align these fragmented pieces of our appetites, feelings, perceptions and beliefs to connect ourselves to one foundation.

The *taqwa* of God.

Many of us perform actions mindlessly to feel certain emotions and to avoid others. A lot of these mindless actions may transform into maladaptive habits and addictions because we choose to not confront the roots of our feelings and emotions. Inner beauty is cultivated through the interrogation of our surroundings and ourselves. Why do we readily accept shifting popularized beauty ideals, "liberatory" narratives and dominate ideologies without questioning their validity? Instead we are questioned and we are often left unable to answer because we don't know ourselves. We don't know what our freedom *looks* like or what beauty *feels* like. Therefore we first need to be present in our emotions, experiences, actions and interactions. Allah calls for this presence and warns us about an entering an illusionary and delusionary state.

"They have hearts with which they do not understand, they have eyes which they do not see, and they have ears which they do not hear. Those are like livestock; rather they are more astray. It is they who are the heedless." – Quran 7:179

If we do not have healthy hearts that are cognizant of the toxicity of external situations, then many times our other senses will be of no use to us. We will continue to live in a state of unconsciousness and therefore we will lack direction. You can have eyes but you will see with an unconscious view and the same is true for hearing.

If you are driving down a road and a cow is blocking your way, the animal will be unperturbed and feel no urgency to move even though he hears and sees the car.

Whereas the distant sound of an engine will be enough to send a squirrel running. The squirrel is conscious because it is mindful of its surroundings and impending dangers. It knows that the car is dangerous to its wellbeing. Therefore the squirrel is self-aware.

Tawqa leads to self-love because taqwa exercises self-awareness. Self-awareness is the first step in cultivating self-love.

Self Justice

"O you who have believed protect yourselves and your families from a Fire.." – Quran 66:6

Contemplating over the choices and events in our lives is important in understanding ourselves in retrospect to our relationship with Allah and His creation. Through this active self-exploration, we look at our *rights* and the *rights* others have upon us. We have a duty to respect. We also have to be aware of the people that dampen our moods and assault our souls.

You cannot be good to others while being unkind to yourself. The ayah above commands us to save ourselves first and then our families. Yourself first. A sleeping person cannot wake another sleeping person up (maybe through snores) but she cannot intentionally awaken anyone. Why? Because she is in an immobile state, she is unconscious herself.

"O you who have believed, be persistently standing firm in justice, witnesses for Allah , even if it be against yourselves or parents and relatives. Whether one is rich or poor, Allah is more worthy of both. So follow not [personal] inclination, lest you not be just. And if you distort [your testimony] or refuse [to give it], then indeed Allah is ever, with what you do, Acquainted." – Quran 4:135

Justice is not asymmetrical; you cannot neglect yourself while being just to others. What you want for others you need to enact it within yourself. Your treatment towards yourself is connected with your own treatment to others. Therefore you will treat others and allow others to treat you the way you treat yourself.

The ayah above commands us to be witnesses for God. In life we often deny, ignore, overlook, excuse and distort the truth. But Allah commands us to be witnesses even if it is against ourselves. Why am I intentionally vomiting up my food after every meal? I am not being just to myself. I have not given myself the right to be healthy and happy in my skin. If you saw a person with bulimia you would console them, advise them to try and move away from this unhealthy practice. But you won't do that for yourself; you won't be a witness to the self-inflicted terrorism that you impose on your own body and mind.

Therefore you are unjust.

When we are just within ourselves, we hold ourselves differently. What we will not tolerate from ourselves we will not tolerate in treatment from other people. This does not mean that we act harshly with others or ourselves. Rather, we are mindful about our lack of honesty with ourselves. With grace and kindness we can steer ourselves away from destructive habits and *advise* others away from toxic choices.

Our injustice to ourselves manifests in what we eat, what we buy, what we watch, in our relationships, what we wear, how much we work, what we read, how much we exercise the list goes on.

To be conscious, means that we are to be consistent in our fight against self-injustice and internal oppression through active presence in the present in order to fully witness our surroundings and actions. If a witness was drunk or mentally impaired in any way during an incident, her testimony may be of no use in the court of law because of the distorted perception caused by the alcohol. Similarly we have to conscious in our lives to see clearly and not mistaken or mislabel love, health and beauty for disrespect, sickness and ugliness.

We are to be the practitioners of God's Teachings of self-love and justice. When you love someone you are honest with him or her. "I love you and so I will not aid in your self destruction."

How we treat each other and ourselves is an indication on how we have prioritized the Divine Teachings. To nurture the seeds of self-love within ourselves we should seek out the Guidance of Al Wadud (the Most Loving). For it is with Him where love is returned, strengthened, nurtured and empowered. It is in this place of strength and clarity where we can offer comfort to others.

Ending Victimhood

Often times, we hold high expectations of other people because they affirm our worthiness and value to ourselves. When they break a promise to us or let us down in some way we become upset and blame them for the cause of our unhappiness. In our minds, we perceived them to be evidences of our right to love and life.

Because we have given others the authority to validate us we look at ourselves through the perception of others. We choose to see through their eyes and we absorb their understandings of what success, happiness, beauty and love look like. And in doing so, we become victims to shifting, contradictory, unhealthy, and many times unrealistic ideals.

Majority, if not all celebrities are victimized in this way. Many politicians, students, doctors, professors, lawyers, nutritionists, activists, super models, imams, priests, rabbis, criminals, addicts, millionaires and billionaires are *victims.*

Victimhood cuts across class, race, religion and professional lines. A lot of times we are not aware that we are mentally enslaved or colonized. Many of us believe that when we escape the material conditions of various stressors such as an abusive relationship or poverty, we have achieved liberatory status. However in many ways we unconsciously and consciously relive and inflict oppression onto others because of the damage done to our thought patterns.

A person who grew up in poverty and becomes a high scale fashion designer, goes on to make overpriced clothing that she wanted to afford when she was young. However she does not interrogate the fact that high fashion maintains its mysticism partly because of its inaccessibility to people who cannot afford these clothing. Why is a dress from the runways in Paris considered to be high fashion compared to a well-made dress from a local seamstress? While she was victimized by class exclusion when she was poor, she now builds her own self-value based on this elitism and therefore perpetuates the hegemonic cultural understanding of haute couture. Her ways of thinking are still oppressed because of her inability to define haute couture in a way that cuts across classism.

Instead of challenging the dominate opinions of class, elegance and sophistication and creating new forms of meaningful beauty narratives, many people choose to not dismantle the structures when they reach the top instead they move within them and continue to reinforce these walls.

Many times, when people engage in plastic surgery they are oppressed and oppressors. They are oppressed because they have been conditioned to view beauty in a certain way and they are oppressors because they are unwilling to liberate themselves from this distorted understanding and thus perpetuate this exclusionist idea of beauty.

When we purchase brand name purses as identity markers of our class status, we are reinforcing the notion that elegance and class are dictated by one social group of people. As *Muslimahs*, we need to create new forms of meaningful beauty paradigms for ourselves. There is tenacity in freedom. Freedom is not a goal that is reached rather freedom is practiced everyday. It involves being able to navigate through the fogginess of racism and classism that keep us immobile in order to assert our humanity and truth.

Many believe that wearing the headscarf is oppressive and wearing less clothing is liberating. But we should question why Western civilization has a monopoly over defining beauty. Why is it always other standards we are trying to live up to?

What are we doing to challenge the cultural distortions and hegemonic understandings of beauty? We need to begin exercising *our freedom* and contemplate on what it means when Allah the Exalted states to us:

"You are the best nation produced [as an example] for mankind. You enjoin what is right and forbid what is wrong and believe in Allah" – Quran 3:110

Struggle and enjoy the process of discovering yourself through your struggle against mental colonization and victimhood. Freedom is a practice that is sustained by action and not necessarily by external change.

Jihad does not equate to suicide bombings, harming innocent people, rape, or an ill conceived, perverse idea of "holy war." Jihad is freedom within *yourself*, it is primarily the struggle against *self imposed* oppression and *internal* enemies. If we address our lack of self-injustice, our lack of consciousness, our victimhood, our enslavement to harmful and unrealistic ideals, we can begin to exercise our inner beauty. The struggle is the wind against our backs not the achievements. Achievements come from Allah the Most High. When we stand before our Lord, we will be judged on how we could have used our skills, bodies, time and minds to the maximum potential. Imagine the adjudication will be according to the best version of ourselves that our circumstances would allow. We have the capacity to try to pray better, eat better, think better and live better and not be oppressed or reinforce destructive cultural paradigms that paralyze us in victim mentality.

"Indeed, Allah will not change the condition of a people until they change what is in themselves." – Quran 13:11

Allah also states:

"And those who strive for Us – We will surely guide them to Our ways. And indeed, Allah is with the doers of good." – Quran 29:69

Inner beauty lies in the struggle not in the materialization of goals. Results are secondary and the struggle is the vehicle of transformation. When you have children, raise them well, do your duty and leave the rest to Allah. Parents often raise them with the goal of producing God loving children but the guidance is not in our hands. Farmers do not control the sun or the rain when planting crops. Leave it to Allah. When trying to lose weight, we should exercise, eat well, be well and leave it to God.

In all actions, do the self-work necessary for freedom and then leave the rest to Allah. Freedom lies in surrender, before, during and after you have done the work to improve your circumstances.

" And upon Allah, Let the believers rely" – Quran 3:160

With this mental surrender, we can enjoy the struggle, we can pay attention to the obstacles around us because our minds and hearts are not attached to the goals but it is in simply striving. Therefore self-actualization is in the present. If you are a broke medical student trying to become a doctor, single parent trying to raise children in the best way, struggling to memorize the Quran, or striving for inner wellness, remember, "Allah is *with* the *doers* of good." – Quran 29:69

Managing Feelings

"Verily, the soul is a persistent enjoiner of evil except for those upon which my Lord has Mercy" – Quran 12:53

We are mired in emotions that can be used to improve our state or worsen our condition. A trait like jealousy often conjures images of evil, greed and malice. However the Prophet stated that jealousy is healthy on two occasions; when we are jealous of a wealthy person who utilizes their resources for beneficial purposes and of a person who has been given knowledge of Allah and they use it for self-improvement and aiding others. (Bukhari) Therefore, it is not the mere presence of wealth or knowledge; rather it is the possibilities of utility. We desire these tools because we want to cultivate inner beauty for ourselves. Therefore envy is aimed at the tools available to exercise beauty and it is not preoccupied with harboring ill feelings of a person simply for the sake of possessing wealth and knowledge.

To be envious of wealth and knowledge in this way requires a level of cognitive consonance. The person who is envious of a wealthy philanthropist for the right reasons is not primarily fixated on the acquisition of cars and homes; rather she looks at money from the angle of spirituality. That the more someone is given, the greater the possibilities to reproduce good. This desire to serve stems from her recognition that "Allah is with the doers of good. " Many times money only exacerbates our internal toxicity because it fuels our addictions, hedonism and greed. To use our resources in ways that are enriching and healthy for ourselves and those around us, we need to be spiritually enriched and maintain this state within ourselves despite the different changes in our lives.

Allah has given us many tools to practice beauty. If we have health we can practice beauty, if we have parents, children, siblings, neighbors we can practice beauty. If we are impoverished, sick or illiterate we can still practice beauty. To self generate beauty requires that we are grateful and patient.

Gratitude is seeing the whole picture, the reality of this *Dunya* and understanding that whatever trials or afflictions we face we will come out of it stronger with resilience, wiser from our experience and lighter from the expiation of some of our sins, God Willing

On the other hand, in order to *be* patient we have to be grateful in that when things are not going our way, it is important to look at all the things that are going right in our lives. If we lost our job, we still have a family, if our hair falls out we still have our health, if we lose our health we still have our faith. It is beneficial to remind ourselves of all the undeserving gifts around us to keep us grounded in our patience.

"If you are grateful, I will surely increase you" – Quran 14:7

Allah does not specify what He will increase us in, which means our lives can be enriched in a plethora of ways. If we practice viewing our circumstances in a positive manner, our minds will experience a decrease in anxiety and sadness. This is one of the many fruits of gratitude in that as our perception changes, we are able to withstand more because of our gratitude.

Our reactions to life's hurdles are what we make them. They can be the fertile soil for our flowers to bloom or they can be the weeds that choke our flowers in our garden for inner beauty. Reactions undermine or facilitate our efforts in cultivating inner beauty. We need to be conscious of how we understand and interpret our situations and circumstances to change our harmful thought patterns and actions. For example, Allah states that

"The servants of the Most Merciful are those who walk upon the earth easily, and when the ignorant address them [harshly], they say [words of] peace" – Quran 25:63

Allah wants us to move away from reactionary anger, from becoming slaves to our temper and from being easy to provoke.

A man said to the Prophet (saw) "Give me advice" The Prophet (saw) said "Do not get angry." The man asked repeatedly and the Prophet answered each time, "Do not get angry." (Bukhari)

Reactionary anger clouds your sense of rationality and leaves you unbalanced. It also sucks you dry of your energy and time. You may say or do something that you would not do in times of ease. You become a slave to your emotions. " Oh I am sorry for the things I said when I was angry" "You know how I get when I am angry" These types of phrases handicap us to our emotions and make our anger as the controller of our intellect rather than the other way around. These types of phrases also make directionless and uncontrollable anger excusable to ourselves and others. When in reality it is an emotion that we can manage with our intellect.

It is often the case that the calm person exercises more control over a situation. They are the most calculated in their words and actions. They see the weakness in a person as the inability to control themselves and they do not engage in that experience. The calm person tries to rectify and if they are unable to do so, they leave. In the process they grow by learning from the experience and what it tells them about the human condition. If someone responds to us rudely, disrespects or hurts us in anyway, we learn something about that individual and we also have to critically examine our actions, our internal thoughts and biases that may have triggered this response from someone else.

When we experience anger, our intense reactions usually come from our lack of personal boundaries on how we love and hate. The Prophet once stated one should love and hate in moderation. (Tirmidhi)

Extreme hate and blind love destroys the individual that harbors such feelings. It leaves them unbalanced and likely to engage in actions that are corrosive to their well-being. For example, were someone to injure your family member, your extreme hatred would not only be directed towards the aggressor, but you would perhaps seek revenge that was disproportionately more harming than what was committed against your family member. You would go as far as maybe seeking to *kill* the aggressor or even harming his loved ones even though they had nothing to do with action. This extreme hatred brought about by anger clouded your sense of reasoning and ultimately lead you to commit actions of injustice. Extreme hatred and love is degrading and unhealthy because we surrender our ability to control our feelings and when we do this we behave in ways that illustrate our powerlessness.

To be in a state of calmness during a conflict requires consciousness and a surety within ourselves. If you are situated and grounded in your beauty, people should not be able to move you out of it. We react in messy ways for many reasons including disrespect. However our honour, dignity and respect are not owned by others and therefore they are unable to take it from us. If you believe that your honour lies with others, then you will dishonor yourself continuously through your reactionary anger or blind obedience to reclaim it. To love moderately, also requires us to manage our feelings. To see the person as what they are and not higher than they are. To not base my self worth on a relationship with a human who is struggling to find and sustain his own self worth. To love moderately, is what allows us to keep our independence and at the same time enjoy interdependence. When we love moderately, we can enjoy growing and lasting relationships and we can forgive easily based on our understanding of the human condition.

When we love and hate in moderation, we will not continue to play the victim in our lives. Many times when we are madly in love, we wait for our partners to save us or to improve our conditions. That is victimhood because you believed that your emotional well-being is based on another's capability to make you happy instead of making yourself content.

When we are stuck in a victim mentality, we blame others for our actions, our sadness, our apathy and our failures. It is easier for us to put blame on someone else or other external conditions because it lifts responsibility from us. However in doing so, mental victimhood keeps us immobile and hands the power of our emotional, mental, physical and spiritual well being to external factors. If we go through something in life, we should not blame our self-neglect as a cause and effect. "I am an alcoholic because of this" or "If I had a good relationship with my mother, I would not be in prison" Victims drag the past with them and soil their future. Redeemers create their future and use the past to develop themselves into stronger human beings.

That is inner beauty, to rise above being slaves to our emotions. To make peace internally when there is war externally. To choose love over pain. You were already *hurt* by someone else why do you continue to *hurt* yourself? Wasn't once enough? It doesn't have to be cause and effect. You can break that pattern.

The goal here is not to get rid of emotions but to learn how to manage, recognize and use emotions to propel us forward. To cultivate inner beauty is to be in touch with how our daily occurrences make us feel and play out into our lives. To ask ourselves, what is this title of victimhood going to do for me currently and in the future? Will I be able to develop the relationships I want, accomplish my dreams and live a purposeful life? Or will I continue to put others in charge of my feelings, self-esteem and actions by my extreme emotions?

To know ourselves is to free ourselves.

Self Awareness

While we work at asserting our internal wellness and begin to feel better, we may start to battle with another inner demon called arrogance. The more internally conscious a person becomes, the more alert they are to imbalances in other people.

We may start to recognize different weaknesses and self harm patterns in others but we should be careful to not delve too deeply in the issues of other people that we forget about ourselves because what happens when someone is too busy looking at and tending to the weeds in someone else's garden? She doesn't realize the weeds slowly growing in her own because of the neglect.

Arrogance is a weed.

It's a weed because in many of us it continuously comes back. Therefore it needs constant supervision and pruning to keep it away. Human beings have enormous potential and at the same time they are also flawed. We lie, cheat, steal, forget, we are weak and we break promises. We let our own selves down all the time, we are bad to ourselves, we oppress ourselves and cheat ourselves by denying ourselves happiness, love, fulfillment and health. And if we do that to our own selves, why do we think we are better than other people? Arrogance is another state of mental victimhood because we allow the perceived weakness in someone else's character influence how we view ourselves. This is manifested when someone states " I am not a *dishonest* person because I cheated on my tax returns at least I am not a habitual liar like my brother." "What I did was not that bad. At least I didn't murder someone." " I am not a *neglectful* parent, at least my kids are not homeless." "I am not a *neglectful* wife at least I make my husband meals. So what if I smoke? At least I am not an alcoholic like her"

These statements illustrate a change in our mental perception in relation to other people's bad choices. You define yourself according to others. Your self-esteem is based on if you are doing better than others.

In this way we stay complacent to our garden full of weeds while scoffing at the neighbor's garden. Suddenly our weeds are not that tall and they are not that plentiful in comparison to the neighbors. But to the outside world, both of our gardens need work.

Victimhood.

Your perception of the neighbor's choices heightened your arrogance, which makes you a victim because of the change in your individual self-awareness. You forget who you are because they forgot who they are. This kind of victimhood often creates pretentious attitudes and an egotistical sense of self worth. It is victimhood because your self-esteem is still derived from external factors.

It is a known fact that when we recognize weaknesses in other people, a few minutes later we are experiencing road rage or we may engage in malicious gossip against a person behind their back. That is human nature, our weaknesses are different but they are still weaknesses. If a person does not have anger issues, maybe she is dishonest. If you are not dishonest, maybe you have anger issues. We are all riddled with internal deficiencies, therefore how can you elevate yourself and place another beneath you? It doesn't matter the class, ethnicity, status or appearance, we are all battling with our own weaknesses. If we understand this, the way we view people changes because we see them on more or less an equal footing with us. That is not to say there are not people who are doing the work necessary for self-actualization and because of this internal work they have reached a stronger level of inner beauty. But because of their self-work, they are to be seen as a *reflection* of what we can be if we put in the same effort. The cultivation of inner beauty is a continual process of self-reflection and choices until our deficiencies become finer and finer.

So what will we *choose?* Will we continue to be reactionary, to be unjust, to be emotionally empty, to be spiritually disconnected from God and ourselves? To be anchored in mental ugliness? Or will we push forward? Change and transform.

Indulgence

"Oh people! Become Muslim, for Muhammad gives as if he has no fear of want..." (Bukhari)

In English the word *Israaf* roughly translates to wasteful extravagance. It is used in various ayat in the Quran to illustrate the tendency of humans to indulge excessively in various activities. We can do *Israaf* with food, clothing, makeup, friends, education, work, sleep, exercising, activism and even worship. While there is nothing inherently destructive in any of the above mentioned, it becomes an issue when we spend an excessive amount of our time focusing solely on these aspects. It is a problem because we become consumed and neglectful of other parts in our lives. Allah states in the Quran that we are a middle community (Quran 2:143) and therefore extremism in anything will disturb this equilibrium. It is easier to fall into extremities than to tightrope through life. However what is easier is usually not the most beneficial and what requires diligence is usually more rewarding and healthy. Many people obtain a fleeting sense of fulfillment through *Israaf.* For example a body builder or an activist may center their lives around one form of self expression. It is what they build their identity on and many times gather their worth from. Other people indulge to distract from personal trauma, anxiety and depression. In this sense engaging in *Israaf* acts as a band aid to a seeping wound and needs to be changed frequently. The band-aid will not make the blood stop running, you are just wasting your time and energy continuously taking off, replacing and rewrapping the gauze. When we engage in *Israaf,* we mentally limit ourselves to focus on one facet of self-expression. It also blinds us to all the other things in our lives that nourish and sustain us. Your sense of self worth cannot be reduced to achievements, purchases, activities and people. Rather these things give a temporary rush of excitement that we should not build our worth on. For example, in many houses, people use decorative lamps even though these lamps are usually not as powerful as the main lights on the ceiling. If the decorative lights were to stop working, it would not be a huge issue because you have a bigger medium of light i.e.; the main ceiling lights. These lamps are just nice decorative items and you do not expect them to do for you what the ceiling lights do for you.

The decorative lamps are the achievements, the clothing and the trophy spouse. While the ceiling light is your own happiness. We need to locate our own exhaustive light within ourselves instead of searching for flashlights or lamps. Look at the real reasons for your overindulgence and extravagance.

Understand that when you spend your money and time wastefully, it does not increase your beauty, intellect, honour or your dignity in the Sight of God. And the attention you do receive, from people is fleeting until they see another individual who has been given more. Take for example, a woman who purchases an expensive jacket, she buys it thinking about all the compliments and attention she will receive from others. However when she wears the jacket, she notices that while she may receive compliments it does nothing to satisfy her being. And in the event that she does not receive compliments or receives very few, she thinks to herself was all that money worth a few words? Does our status depend on how others think of how we look or speak, or how many places we travel to or how many restaurants we visit?

The phenomenon of social media illustrates that we are in an age of extravagance by creating and projecting images for the visual consumption of others. Essentially, we are living for others within the box of success that they have constructed.

Allah tells us that we should *"Know that the life of this world is but amusement and diversion and adornment and boasting to one another and competition in increase of wealth and children" – Quran 57:20*

And while we are active on various websites, images of celebrities and opulence, play upon our insecurities and make us feel unhappy or unsatisfied with what we have been blessed with by Allah. We are constantly reminded of what we do not have and what is wrong with our hair, skin and bodies in order to purchase more items. Moreover the popularity of make up artists in the recent years, perpetuate the belief that we cannot be beautiful for free. We have to buy lashes, lipstick, eyebrow palettes and foundations. And the pictures posted online depicting the before and after the makeup tutorials, reinforce the commodification of beauty. The practice of contouring noses to make them look thinner and less flat reinforces the distortion beauty. In addition to decorating our faces, we alter our features in ways that mimic surgical procedures. As we contour, we subconsciously agree with racist beauty ideals that are exclusionist on a theoretical front and also class segregated. In that many makeup companies align themselves with the economic spending power of those who are affluent. If we look at the most popular and the most advertised makeup products, they are usually more expensive and carried in higher end department stores. This covertly suggests that women with contoured cheekbones and noses are to be seen as classier and more elegant than women who choose to go without wearing makeup. Moreover, many of the makeup models in advertisements are of similar racial background and therefore these ads subtly intertwine, class and race when presenting beauty narratives.

The positioning of these products in the socio spatial sense by the location of their availability reinforces the idea that beauty is associated with class status. This distorted understanding of beauty will continue to be sustained by the restless spending habits of the marginalized, the underrepresented, the poor and working class who instead of challenging and creating new expressions of beauty have accepted this commercialized and elitist understanding.

It is *who* holds the power of culture production that defines *what* is in and *who* is in.

The makeup industry exploits our insecurities and profits off our distorted perceptions of beauty. So we spend. And the masks we paint on our faces are the same ones we wear to sell dreams and illusions of happiness.

We have become a society of extravagance. We over eat, over sleep, over work , over spend and the list goes on. In surah Az Zumar we are told, "O My Servants, who have transgressed against themselves do not despair of the Mercy of Allah. Indeed, Allah forgives all sins. Indeed it is He Who is Forgiving, the Merciful" – Quran 39: 53

It is interesting to note that Allah used the word '*asrafoo*' which is associated with the word of *israaf* meaning that what was done in excess was against ourselves. When we go overboard in anything, we do it against ourselves even if we think that what we are over indulging in is to our own benefit. When you over ate it wasn't benefitting you. When you bought that dress that was way over your financial means, it did not benefit you. When you stayed in that toxic relationship, it was not in your best interests. Rather it was corrosive to your wellbeing.

But even after all of the times that we have wronged our own souls, Allah commands us to *not* despair in losing His Mercy. Our Lord promises that He forgives all sins if we submit ourselves to Him. If we stop can stop chasing the mirage of happiness and work towards the real thing.

Islam does not call for austerity, however it calls for us to live and enjoy the bounties of life consciously. To live a balanced life within our financial, health, spiritual and intellectual means.

"Oh you who have believed, respond to Allah and to the Messenger when he calls you to that which you gives you life." – Quran 8:24

Life is not needless debt, it is not misery and not to be wasted by chasing temporary fixes to unhappiness. God is calling you to a life that transcends unbridled acquisition, materialism and consumerism. We are enough as we are, without the excess and Islam pushes us to redefine our definition of happiness. Truly honour, status and esteem belong to Allah but self-actualization, happiness and satisfaction lies with Him also.

Remembering Allah

"And be not like those who forgot Allah, so He made them forget themselves." – Quran 59:19

Who is God and what would feel like to be in His Presence? As Muslims we know that there is nothing or any being that resembles or is comparable to Him. Therefore our minds are incapable of conjuring up any visuals because when we try, we only produce images that we already have seen. The words beauty, wealth, power and honour invoke memories of realities that we have experienced in our lives. However, when speaking of Allah's Beauty, Richness, Power and Honour we have nothing to compare it against because we have never seen anything that has Beauty, Richness, Power and Honour like

Allah. Moreover, when we speak about the Names and Attributes of Allah such as the Wise, the Generous, the Compassionate, the Appreciative, the Loving and the Merciful, we find that He possesses Attributes that we would want in a friend, in a mother, a father, a sibling and in any life companion. Fortunately for us, these Attributes of God are perfect and lasting. His is a Love that is flawless, fulfilling and complete, His is a Compassion that is encompassing over all areas of life. His Provisions are given without even asked and many times even thanked. And Because He is the Most Wise, Allah has knowledge of the future, present and the past. He knows what will happen to you in the grave, what would happen if you went right or left. If you went to a different school or if you married that individual. If you never got sick, if you never lost a loved one or if you were to get that job. Couple this sweeping Wisdom with perfect Love, that is free from any type of flaws, we see that Allah holds the perfect Guidance and is the ultimate Source of Strength and Peace. And because He is Unique in His Perfection, every other source including ourselves is imperfect and flawed in their friendship, love, advice and protection. It is important to understand that, we are not without purpose or direction. We exist to know Allah through ourselves, the Quran, His Miracles even through other people. For some of us, it is through the imperfection of others, that we come to realize the Perfection of our Lord. We have all been hurt, disappointed and betrayed. We have experienced abuse, neglect and toxicity from people who have said that they loved us. We have had loved ones change, leave us and die. And because of this, we often find it hard to love completely and deeply.

We are looking for a perfect love that is enriching, fulfilling and lasting in a world that is none of these things. Your Lord's Love is not confided by or bounded to time, space or thought. The Love of Allah does not only fill the crevices within the human heart, but it over flows and seeps through the walls of its chambers carrying on through our deaths and afterlives.

Engaging in a duel loving relationship with Allah requires remembrance. (*Dhikr*) It is this remembrance that illuminates and guides us through the fogginess we experience in our lives and uplifts us despite our circumstances. It is in this remembrance where we are given the freedom to love and live. We realize with the Love of Allah we don't have to wait for anything or anyone to add to our lives and we don't have to acquire anything to be enough or to feel beautiful. It is in this reverence of Allah where we can reclaim our lives, our minds and souls. Perhaps the most beautiful part, is that practicing our love for Allah is easily accessible, in that it begins with simply an internal choice to experience what it means to practice love and to be loved. And because you never reach the end of loving Allah there is no need for higher spiritual love.

When an individual is preoccupied with this remembrance, she can become a friend of God. *InshaAllah,* with Dhikr, we can enter a realm where we exercise love and receive Divine love continuously.

The Prophet stated, "*When Allah loves a slave, calls out Jibril and says: 'I love so-and-so; so love him'. Then Jibril loves him. After that he (Jibril) announces to the inhabitants of heavens that Allah loves so-and-so; so love him; and the inhabitants of the heavens (the angels) also love him and then make people on earth love him". (Bukhari)*

Allah informs Jibril of His love for an individual and Jibril informs the people of Paradise of the identity of the one whom Allah loves. Because when the All Mighty loves a person, the angels and the inhabitants of Paradise are informed, then the world should know that you love Allah. The way you treat yourself, parents, children, spouse, animals, the environment, co-workers, orphans, elderly, and teachers should reflect the reverence you have for your Lord. When a person is in love they are changed in the way they think, walk and talk. That is how the Love of Allah should change us.

When a slave remembers her purpose in relation to the Divine, she *inshaAllah* will be engaged in performing actions that generate, beauty and recognition from the Lord of the Universe. Consequently, when He loves her, the inhabitants of the world will only follow suit. And they will love her whether she looks like a supermodel or a burn victim. The Love of Allah is not superficial and it is given to slaves that emanate beauty and light in the true sense. Therefore to strengthen this relationship, we must begin to exercise our Remembrance of Allah.

So what does remembering Allah look like?

To remember Allah means living a fulfilled and enriched life. When we remember and earnestly strive to gain Allah's Love, our daily actions will align with our purpose for existence. "I did not create the Jin and Man except that they Worship Me." – Quran 51:56 It is with this alignment, that we can achieve success and live a healthy and liberating life.

Many times in this world we see that jealousy and abuse are mislabeled as love. For example, take butterfly catchers who capture, kill and preserve butterflies for their beauty. Consequently many butterfly species are endangered partly because of this hedonistic desire to posses and contain beauty. However, this is the antithesis of love because true love fosters growth and beauty and encourages health and happiness of both parties. True love is a duel relationship and not an asymmetrical association of oppressed and oppressor. So while we are engaged in searching for this type of love, we have to examine ourselves to see if we are producing this type of love. For ourselves and each other. Sometimes our love is flawed because that is all we know. So when we mislabel cruel, degrading and neglectful behavior as love, this illustrates our ignorance of love and self-love. This is usually evident in our own treatment of ourselves as we are often the first victims of our ignorance about love.

How you hold yourself, is telling on how much you love God. You are as loved as you allow yourself to be. If you practice love towards Allah you will be a paradigm for self-love and inner beauty.

For centuries, women have been victimized from others and this abuse has influenced their own personal treatment towards their bodies, minds and souls. Muslim women have been told by a countless number of people, religious leaders, governments, institutions, organizations and medical professionals of what self-love, love, of God, beauty, success and happiness look like. That is partly the reason why we see many women poisoning and deforming themselves in efforts to keep up with various interpretations of so-called self-enlightenment.

In the process many Muslim women and many women often end up living inauthentic lives. It is similar to putting on shoes that are way to small and discarding shoes that fit you just because everyone tells you that the smaller size shoes *look* better even though they don't *feel* better. And as we struggle to walk in these shoes, we announce to the world that we have finally become self actualized, hoping that no one sees the disingenuous smiles that mask our pain from the discomfort of our toes being crammed into shoes too tight.

Concepts such as Islamic Feminism, Muslim environmentalists and Modern Muslims illustrate that we have begun to mentally disassociate from Islam. When we use additional adjectives to describe the type of Muslim we are, we subconsciously reinforce to ourselves and others the misconception that Islam is deficient. In that we need to be Islamic Feminists to be considered pro women. It is not enough to be Muslim. However, if we knew Allah and we knew our Prophet, we would not need titles of disassociation and identification such as Feminist and Modernist. If we knew what the Guidance of Allah looks like, we would understand that it is complete and encompassing for both genders and that it is timeless and context specific to our needs, our situations and our lives. Instead of trying to reconcile Islam with dominate ideologies, we would see that it is not the essence of our religion that needs to change rather we need to interrogate ourselves and ideologies, interpretations and narratives that are espoused by Muslims and non-adherents for their validity and truth.

For example, one of the ways in which critics attack Islam is on its supposed misogynistic and puritanical representation of women. The question of purity and a woman's honour in Islam has been misunderstood and misinterpreted. It is important to note, that purity, is not limited to the chastity of women. Rather purity is related to a plethora of activities including the maintenance of inner well-being. Allah tells us that this inner well-being will be our saving grace on the Day of Judgment.

"The Day when there will not benefit [anyone] wealth or children. But only one who comes to Allah with a sound heart." – Quran 26:88-89

Both men and women have the same responsibility to live in a purified manner and their choices can bring about their own unhappiness. Therefore a woman's purity is equated to her purity as a worshipper and connection with her Lord. The same is true for a man.

What we should concern ourselves with, is the practice of purity in all aspects of our lives. For example when we keep our bodies, minds, and souls clean and groomed we should do so because *"Allah loves those who purify themselves" – Quran 9:108*

As is well known, people have distorted meanings of what a pure woman looks like.

"The Prophet informed that, "Allah once forgave a prostitute. She passed by a dog panting near a well. Seeing that thirst had nearly killed him, she took off her shoe, tied it to her scarf, and drew up some water. Allah forgave her for that." (Bukhari)

This hadith speaks to the God given ability within humans to assert their humanity by doing actions of meaningful connection with other living beings.

We are often told of the many obstacles in our spiritual path towards God and that is why many who have committed prohibited actions are hopeless when trying to cultivate a relationship with God. Many would consider a prostitute to be devoid of the human qualities that can bring about self-awareness and choose to instead view the prostitute as an object rather than a thinking and living being.

In the above hadith narration, we see that the woman earns a living through self-deprecation. In essence her food, her clothing and substance is nourished through degrading means. However, through an act of kindness and humanity in connecting with other living beings Allah bestows mercy on her. We can transcend our current state without dragging our past with us to claim the beauty of our future.

In that, a prostitute yesterday can be one of the most dignified people in the world today through her humanity and active practice of beauty and worship *Fee Sabililah.* Self invention is not contingent on our current status. Which is why we do not ascribe purity to ourselves. It is what we are after everyday as a process, but it is granted to us not achieved. Therefore we should not let others dissuade us about God's Acceptance of us when we try to live healthier lives. They project their limited view of Allah's Mercy on to us, when in reality human beings cannot monopolize the Mercy of God. That is why the imagination is integral in the worship of Allah because what we believe we shall aspire to become. If you believe that Allah will forgive you, you will act in ways that affirm this belief and improve your condition. We are reminded about the vastness of the Mercy of Allah in the following hadith;

"There was a man from Bani Israel who murdered ninety-nine persons. Then he set out asking (whether his repentance could be accepted or not). He came upon a monk and asked him if his repentance could be accepted. The monk replied in the negative and so the man killed him. He kept on asking till a man advised him to go to such and such village. (So he left for it) but death overtook him on the way. While dying, he turned his chest towards that village (where he had hoped his repentance would be accepted), and so the angels of mercy and the angels of punishment quarreled amongst themselves regarding him. Allah ordered the village (towards which he was going) to come closer to him, and ordered the village (whence he had come), to go far away, and then He ordered the angels to measure the distances

between his body and the two villages. So, he was found one span closer to the village (he was going to). So he was forgiven." (Bukhari)

Because the Monk told the man that it was fruitless to repent, he mentally immobilized this man to his present conditions. With the second encounter we see that we are to see past the present conditions of an individual, to view the possibilities and expansiveness of Allah's Mercy. In our journey towards self-growth, we are to *create* new paradigms of redemptive healing when there are none available to mirror. That is why the imagination is crucial in worshiping Allah because it is important to imagine and hope differently despite what everyone else tells you. His belief and hope in Allah, teaches us to not live under someone else's gaze and to *enact* what you first *envision* to *be* Allah's Mercy. Perhaps you are closer to God's Love than you think but your mind has to be there before your body is.

When speaking of status, it is important to mention the importance of Bilal ibn Rabah as one of the companions of the Prophet. Bilal was of African descent and an emancipated slave. The racialization and politicization of black bodies was evident during the Prophetic period and mirrored the racist social structures that existed. Upon hearing about Bilal's reversion to Islam, his "owner" Ummayah ibn Khalaf, tortured and nearly killed him, ordering him to renounce his faith.

This idea of the slave being property meant the refusal for a slave to form any identity that was different or conflicting to that of the master's. In that there was an insistence to be a hallowed version of a human, one without a sense of roots, uniqueness and beliefs. To be a slave meant that you were rooted in the present, and your past and future were not yours. A slave today was always going to be a slave tomorrow.

However, his reversion to Islam illustrated that while his body may not have legally belonged to him, his mind did. And Bilal's mental agency was materialized with his physical emancipation. His emancipation made his innate freedom into something that could now be seen in the legal sense.

However, even if he was not emancipated, Bilal affirmed his humanity the day he accepted Islam because he exercised his ability of *choice* despite the fact that he was going against the slavery establishment and its pervasive insistence on his subjection and mental colonization. Bilal represents the black and oppressed experience for many descendants of slaves and oppressed people because his story is one of courage and redemption in the face of racism and oppression.

Despite his perceived inferiority due to his blackness and slave status, Allah took him to the top (quite literally) as he stood on top of the most revered and Holiest site to the Arabs, the Kaba to make the call to prayer. There is an instance, recorded in the Hadith books that narrates that the Prophet asked Bilal;

"Bilal, tell me which act you did at the time of the morning prayer for which you hope to receive good reward, for I heard during the night the sound of your footsteps before me in Paradise?" (Muslim)

Bilal may have been considered to be inferior by the societal standards of those times, however his status with God was significant.

Out of all the things that the Prophet could have seen, all the information he could have collected about any of his companions, Allah magnified Bilal's status to the Prophet and to billions of others who would come across the above narration in the future. With the example of Bilal, we are presented a decolonized image of what beauty looks like.

Heroism, beauty and self-actualization do not come in one aesthetic. We see various types of women in the Quran that displayed tremendous amounts of courage, patience and beauty in their character. Allah the All Mighty shows us with the example of Bilal and other luminous figures that greatness comes in many different forms including in your image. Self-actualization cuts across class, gender and ethnicity and our heroes can look like us and people from all walks of life.

In essence there is no one better, than she who does the internal self-work necessary for inner wellness and invites others to do the same. The inner awakening is what anchors us and keeps us from being thrown off balance at every situation. When you have a purpose, everything that comes to you, will be used as either fuel to get to the goal or it will be avoided. Things, Ideas, Thoughts, behaviors and even people can be avoided if they are obstructing your path to self-love. In this sense, beauty requires, awareness, action and vigilance. True beauty does not mean extremism, hate, murder, forced marriages or terrorism. It also does not mean war, infidelity, consumerism, usury, gluttony, laziness, arrogance and abuse.

These are by products of unhealthy, unbalanced and neglected souls. When people harm other people, it is a reflection of their own self-harm and neglect. The soul projects what it is and produces what it knows. How can you expect a snake to produce anything but venom?

One action that can be seen as a symptom of this inner poison is backbiting.

Allah States:

"O you who have believed, avoid much (negative) assumption. Indeed, some assumption is sin. And do not spy or backbite each other. Would one of you like to eat the flesh of his brother when dead? You would detest it. And fear Allah ; indeed, Allah is Accepting of repentance and Merciful." – Quran 49:12

In the passage above, God likens backbiting to consuming a corpse, illustrating the repugnance of the action.

How can someone maintain their dignity when they are willingly consuming a decaying human corpse? And on top of that, the flesh of their sibling. There is no saving grace in this situation, no space for excuses or reasons. This intentional violence desecrates the human body of the one who is consumed and the consumer.

That is the comparison of slander and rumors. There is no beauty in the action and the actress only poisons herself as she ingests the putrid flesh of her sibling.

Yet we have magazines and shows that make millions from the business of cannibalism. The very livelihood of the paparazzi are built on spying, harassment and suspicion.

It is easier and less painful, to focus on other people and it is also more crippling.

The practice of remembering Allah does the opposite in that it forces us to interrogate ourselves about our weaknesses and wrestle with the shortcomings of our own souls. The taqwa of Allah leads us on a path of self-development, a path that requires, patience and courage. We say courage because it is not easy to critically examine and face ones flaws objectively. Moreover, when we remember Allah, our interpretations of events will be self-affirming rather than disempowering. For example, if we become sick, someone who remembers Allah will interpret the illness as an opportunity for the expiation of her sins and an opportunity to become closer to Allah. This empowering interpretation of the illness allows her to be optimistic and at peace. On the other side, a person who has a disempowering interpretation of the sickness may fall into depression through worrying and complaining over her fate. She may tell herself, that I am sick because I am bad and she is healthy because she is good. One who remembers Allah, will remember that she cannot always assume that someone has high or low status with Allah because of their ease or hardship because everything is a test. Health, sickness, wealth and poverty are all tests.

For example in Surah Al Kahf, we learn that an arrogant man was given two gardens and a believing couple experienced the death of a child. We cannot assume the status of people because of what they posses or "lack" in this life. How we respond to our own battle is telling of our inner beauty and our relationship with Allah.

As humans, we are created with enormous potential and also great weaknesses.

The Prophet (saw) said, *"Jannah is nearer to anyone of you than your shoe-lace, and so is the (Hell) Fire." (Bukhari)*

We are at a proximal distance to both self-destruction and self-actualization, illustrating the ease in which we oscillate between fulfillment and emptiness. The key that facilitates our growth is our capacity of endurance. The Quran indicates that human beings are created in hardship and all of us will have to face some form of difficulty in our lives. However, when we look at many great people in history, it was under stress, humiliation and sadness where the world witnessed their strength, tenacity and greatness. When we supplicate to God to make us capable believers, who we are today and who we want to be have to be connected by a bridge called experience. There is no teacher more effective than experience, even though we hate her. But if it were not for experience and the vivid lessons of pain, we would not know the meaning of intense joy. When we look at that Year of Sadness for the Prophet, the nature of the death of his wife was largely brought about by her acceptance of Islam and the death of his uncle within the same year meant a loss of protection against community leaders who wanted to harm him. To add to this, the Muslims were oppressed and killed with impunity and the Prophet was harassed and even stoned. With all of this on his shoulders, imagine the constant weariness, the fear, the sadness and yet it was around this period in which Allah chose to take His Prophet to the Heavens where he was shown the splendor, grandeur and exhilaration of Paradise. Isn't it interesting that the Prophet's Year of Sadness was experienced alongside with one of the most glorious moments in his life?

That is the paradox of life, to experience pain at such intensity that it sling shots your potential for growth and knowledge of the meaning of joy. When the heart is enflamed with tribulations, the anxiety, pain and sadness push the emotional boundaries of the heart, so much so that when joy is experienced it is felt at a deeper and heightened level.

We cannot give meaning to happiness without sadness, to relief without pain, to hardship without ease. Therefore when you ask for greatness, take it, take all of it the good and the bad. And remember Allah throughout the challenges. For it will introduce you to you. Allah will introduce you to you.

"Indeed with hardship comes ease." – Quran 94:5

Loving Allah

"You will be with whom you love" – *Prophet of God. (Bukhari)*

Love shapes, guides and gives meaning to our lives. It is with love that we are connected through our minds and hearts. Love is a reflection of who we are, what we desire, and what we hold to be valuable. It is a central experience for our humanity and the *raison d'etre* of our existence.

"And I did not create the jinn and mankind except to worship Me."
– – Quran 51:56

Worship is love at its zenith. When you worship someone you have taken them as your point of reverence, esteem and devotion. The one whom you worship is the highest representation of virtue, even defines the very meaning of goodness for you. Worship is physically manifested on the limbs, however it is born and emanates from the heart. Essentially, whom you love, defines who you are and outlines what you aspire to become.

God created us to experience love and to be loved right back.

Allah invites us to experience a love that changes us but simultaneously allows us to hold on to the best qualities of ourselves. To Love Allah teaches us *how* to love. Because to love, without knowing how to love brings about self harm. At its best, love is transformative as it changes the heart that harbors it and brings beauty forth into its surroundings.

To cultivate beauty and freedom in our lives, it is important to *love* God. You may be saying to yourself, I already love Allah, more than my children, my parents and myself. However love is not a measurement, just because you love Allah more than yourself does not necessarily mean you *love* Allah. Rather we say that I love Allah and therefore I love myself. The love of Allah is what we base our understanding on. If you love God, then you will love. Loving Allah, positions us to view the world and our experiences differently. Loving Allah looks through lenses of truth and not idealism. Love enriches our understanding and allows us to live from the Perspective of the Divine.

"And when I love him, I am his hearing with which he hears, his seeing with which he sees, his hand with which he strikes, and his leg with which he walks..." – Hadith Qudsi; (Bukhari)

We often attempt to substitute or mistaken love for quick rushes of excitement only to quickly cascade into boredom, disappointment and resentment. As finite creatures, many understand love to be something that will wear out and eventually die with time as humans do. However, the Love of Allah stands in contrast to this understanding because we are presented with a Love that is constructed to last and endure. Because this Love demands active participation, we find it easier to stay in our unsatisfying and short-lived experiences instead of feeling real Love. The Love of Allah is not bounded to or defined by time and space rather it is one that triumphs and endures through the temporal structures of this world and carries on to the next. To practice your love for Allah you are essentially etching your name in eternity.

Loving Allah redefines our relationships and attachments. To enter into the space of loving and living for Allah, we learn to live in the present moment and allow ourselves to experience our current emotions in their fullness. When we are present in our lives, we do not live in our dreams for the future or in our memories of the past. Rather we live for today because that is the greatest tool of development.

The present is all we have.

If you completed the Quran yesterday, what are you doing today? If you built a mosque yesterday, what charity are you giving today? If you were good to your parents, neighbors and relatives yesterday, what are you doing today? The present moment allows for the fluidity of self-development and expression. It does not hold us in the past nor preoccupy us with the future. To love Allah means that we focus on the present so much so that we will feel like we live for a day everyday.

But how can we love someone we don't know?

Many times in life, we are faced with trials and we wonder where is the Help of Allah? If we don't know Allah we won't understand the brilliant ways in which He shows His Love to us. For example, if you experience a divorce, it may be difficult to see the beauty in a broken marriage and family. Perhaps through this divorce you will lead a happier and healthier life in the future. You may become stronger and learn weaknesses about yourself that you never knew. One may argue, that Allah can make me stronger and healthy and happy without the divorce. There is nothing that Allah cannot do but He does as He *Wills.* Loving Him is on His terms, He chooses the way in which He manifests His Love to you and it is always in your benefit. And in doing so, we are taught how to trust and to not live in fear of the unknown;

"If Allah intends good for someone, then He afflicts him with trials." – Prophet of God (Bukhari)

If a person were to harm us we would believe that the aggressor's motivations for assaulting us was because of their dislike towards us. People extend this kind of thinking to Allah's Decree, *"But when He tries him and restricts his provision, he says, "My Lord has humiliated me." – Quran* 89:16 You think that your misfortune is a deliberate form of humiliation from Allah. You do not ponder o possibility that Allah is showing you Love throug. event. You do not think that perhaps God is purifying or He is teaching you through this experience or that H strengthening you.

"Allah the Most High said, "I am as My servant thinks of Me, and I am with him if he remembers Me..."- Prophet of God (Bukhari)

If you think that the challenges in your life are *only* manifestations of humiliation and the anger of God, then that is how you will engage in a relationship with Allah. Everything that happens to you will affirm this belief and will guide your interactions and shape your relationships. You will be anxious when facing circumstances at work, school and home. You will be distrustful in your relationships with people because you will believe Allah is using other people to punish you. You will no longer see the beauty in your life but rather your vision will be clouded with your pessimism. Your opinion of Allah will influence your opinion of the world. That is why we say when you *love* Allah, you learn *how* to love because optimism begins with your opinion of your Lord. And since He is the owner and controller of everything, your challenges will be viewed from this love perspective. Of course there are times when Allah, places hardships in our paths because of our sins but He does so to teach us, to grow from our experiences and to not stay in depression and pessimism.

Therefore, to *know* Allah is to *Love* Him, and to Love Him is to *live.*

Because, I believe that Allah is Strong, Wise, Kind and Patient, I can trust His Decree. Moreover, I can trust myself to practice those traits as well.

To know Allah, allows us to move through ease and difficulty with a sense of fluidity. In that, times are not permanent and we do not get attached to hard or easy periods. Also because Allah is permanent, we try to keep our love for Him concrete irrespective of our circumstances.

Compassion, Kindness, Mercy and Love are just a handful of Allah's many Attributes. What is more is that while someone may posses these characteristics he or she does not posses them in their perfection. Take for example that of kindness, it is very difficult to be kind in every situation and when we die, no matter how kind we were during our lifetimes, we cannot be kind in our graves because of our lack of capacity. But Allah is Kind in all situations, even in our tests and many of the situations we perceive to be our misfortunes are embedded with Divine Kindness. We have to repudiate the idea that because Allah tests us this means He does not love us. We have to recognize and look for the love wherever we are and use our present conditions as tools of redemptive healing.

Loving Others *Fee Sabilillah*

The Prophet saw said: "Allah will ask on the Day of Judgment: 'Where are those who loved each other for the sake of My glory? Today, - on a day when there is no shade but Mine… I shall shade them with My shade…." (Muslim)

Love is the most universal and transcendental emotion that unites human beings to act in ways that perhaps they wouldn't otherwise. To love and to be loved is the purpose behind many of the relationships we form in our lifetime. It is also perhaps the most mistaken, abused and ill-defined idea. Many people use the word in ignorance, in that they do not properly understand what it means to love and to be loved. How do we love? And Who do we love?

We love our parents, siblings, children and friends. We feel happy in their presence and we try to be mindful of their feelings and wellbeing. However in numerous places in the Quran, we are told that human beings can be ungrateful (17:67) unjust (14:34) anxious, (70:19) weak (4:28) among other things. The Lord of All that exists has described His creation in these sweeping qualities to illustrate that as flawed human beings we will be disappointed in each other on numerous occasions. An imperfect being can only love imperfectly. Even our love to the Creator is plagued with mistakes. Therefore how should we love each other? For the sake of Allah.

We often hear Muslims saying to one another, I love you *Fee Sabililah* or I love you for the sake of Allah. But what does that mean? How do we love someone for the sake of Allah and not for his or her own sake?

Our religion encompasses even the most intimate feelings between human beings because we are to be conscious of Allah during these expressions. In that when we love, we are mindful of our Lord. And with this mindfulness, we are conscious of our independence in relationships and our healthy codependence. When we are conscious we do not mis-label love and we love rationally in a balanced way. Loving for the Sake of God respects autonomy and codependency because it reminds us that while we are in a loving relationship we are still separate beings. This autonomy within our relationships encourages us to not mask our true selves to impress others and it does not encourage us to remain in the *shadow* of our beloved by absorbing their dreams, values and hopes as our own and sacrificing ours simply because we love them. If we accept this shadow mentality, it will leave an imprint on our subconscious and manifest itself in different ways. For example, we may push our own sacrificed dreams and hopes onto our children because we believe that they should become idealized illusions of themselves to impress others as we did before them. But your children do not exist to abate your anxieties about your unaccomplished goals nor do they exist to fill your thirst for status. We do not exist to serve someone else's fantasy about love, we exist to know love and be loved *as we are.* In many relationships women change their appearances, opinions and values to sustain relations with men who only wish to mold the relationship in their image. Both of these parties do not understand that love is a celebration of both individuality and togetherness. So we should not exercise, dress up and put makeup only to get a man's attention. True love comes to us to as we are and encourages us to develop self-awareness. Relationships are to be used to become more conscious human beings for ourselves.

We cannot mold a person to our liking in order to affirm to us our status, worthiness or fantasies of what love should look like. We should already know our value. Nor should we present a polished and idealized illusion of who we are while concealing our real selves. We should be comfortable with our true selves.

When a plant is watered the water is not aimed at the leaves, rather it is aimed at the soil in order to nourish the roots of the plant. The shiny green leaves come as result of the healthy roots. We often focus on the green leaves (external), forgetting that the love (water) was never aimed at the leaves rather it directed its energies to the root of the plant the part we cannot see. Love is a connection between souls and after it transforms the inner workings of an individual, it radiates outwards. Loving *Fee Sabililah,* says yes, I see you for you, as God created you.

We also see the kindness, beauty and love practiced by others towards us as manifestation of God's Will.

When someone is kind to us, Allah has created his or her heart to function in that way, in our favour. In the event that you are going to visit a doctor and you make *dua* that the doctor is pleasant, patient and informative. When you arrive you find that the doctor is all of the above because it was Allah who made the doctor act that way towards you. You notice, this particular doctor who is nice to you during the time you are with him or her, is dismissive and rude towards other patients who are just as sick as you but Allah influenced their behavior to be pleasant towards only you. Therefore you do not exonerate this doctor from his bad treatment towards other patients, but you recognize that during the period of your checkup Allah pacified the doctor for your sake.

Many times, He is the One driving people's disposition towards us. That is not to say if someone is unkind to you, Allah does not love you because we see the Prophet was abused. Rather when people are kind to us, it is ultimately

Allah who subconsciously prompts them to treat us in that way.

On the other side, when someone is propelled by the desire to be loved by God, they will act in ways that are especially beautiful towards other humans. They will exercise the four virtues of courage, temperance, prudence and justice to the best of their ability. This desire to be loved by Allah, teaches us how to transcend above our appetites, insecurities and fears and in doing so we become embodied paradigms of self love that inspire people to wrestle with their own existential anxieties.

"The Prophet saw said "If I were to take an intimate friend, I would take Abu Bakr. But what binds us is the brotherhood of Islam and its love."

We see the way in which the Prophet expressed his love for people was by always putting the Love of Allah first and loving people through the lens of this spiritual awakening.

In that, the Prophet's closest Friend was God and he loved Abu Bakr for his continual exercise of spiritual wellness. That is what united them, the love of God and the desire to live a purposeful life. When we examine the comradery between them, we see that they both loved and lived for a meaningful purpose.

Because their relationship was based on Divine Teachings, the Prophet and Abu Bakr practiced beauty with each other by exercising their spirituality. What their brotherhood illustrates is that health attracts health. What you embody you will naturally incline towards. Abu Bakr strived to cultivate inner beauty and therefore he deeply loved and admired the Prophet whose devotion to his Lord demonstrated his beauty. Friendship is the springboard for creativity, self-growth and joy. It is the mirror in which you are introduced to yourself by another. It is a bond that exists *outside* yourself but highlights your strengths *within* yourself. Sometimes people's belief in you strengthens your belief in yourself. The relationship with Allah is pivotal in understanding our place within the world and Allah uses different mediums to facilitate our development and give meaning to our lives. When the Prophet first experienced the angel Gabriel, he shakily confided to his wife over what he saw. Khadija replied that he was someone of extraordinary character who was kind to the less fortunate in society. Many years after she died, the Prophet expressed that *"her love is instilled in my heart..."*(Muslim) Her love played a pivotal role in lifting the spirits of the Prophet. Revolutionary love can free us from bondage and awaken our inner consciousness. The fruits of a true love manifests in changes in the person's attitude and thought patterns. A healthy relationship acts us the buffer against the incessant criticism, indifference and conflict that one may face from others. But perhaps more importantly, it lifts us above our own self-doubt and insecurities. A true relationship is the beginning of seeing ourselves authentically.

"The likeness of a righteous friend and an evil friend is the likeness of a (musk) perfume seller and a blacksmith. As for the perfume seller, he may either bestow something on you, or you may purchase something from him, or you may benefit from his sweet smell. And as

for the blacksmith, he may either burn your clothes, or you may be exposed to his awful smell." – Prophet of God. (Bukhari)

When we have companions who exercise beautiful character, their behavior rubs off on us as we spend our time with them. Sometimes when we embrace a scented woman, her perfume lingers on our clothing long after our meeting. The scent is a consequence of the embrace. Similarly, personality adjustments and changes in our mindsets are affected by the time spent in healthy relationships. To love someone for Allah's Sake is to use the relationship as a means of cultivating inner beauty. This means everything you do for each other, the time spent, the advice given, the gifts exchanged the secrets kept all of it is to exercise divinely inspired beauty for His Sake.

In life people often make friends for disingenuous and selfish reasons. It is common that friendships these days are based on opportunistic impulses and exploitation. Therefore people can be friends with others primarily for their wealth, status or job. However those who love each other for the sake of Allah do not seek to use you, or to get anything out of you. When they do us a favour, they do not count the amount of times they did it for us. This is because the reason, the *raison d'etre* for their presence in our lives is to develop a consciousness of their Lord. They seek to strengthen the beauty that is within them.

So when they practice beauty towards us it is for Allah's Sake and when they seek to develop a relationship with you it is because they seek the Companionship of

Allah through you. Their health is inclined to the beauty within you.

We want those types of friends but more importantly we need to *be* those type of friends. When we become the type of friend we would like to have, it is inevitable that Allah will bless us with true gems.

"And those who believe and do righteous deeds, We will surely admit them among the righteous" – Quran 29:9

"O Allah, I ask You for Your love, the love of those who love You, and the actions that make me attain unto Your love. O Allah, make the love of You more beloved to me than my self, my family..." (Tirmidhi)

Part 2: Loving Yourself Fee Sabililah; Enhancing Physical Beauty

True beauty is cultivated in knowing and loving Allah which will in turn enable us to flourish physically, emotionally and spiritually. Loving ourselves *Fee Sabililah,* entails that we should be the primary beneficiaries of our own beauty. Many times in life, we find that we do so much for others and we don't have any energy or desire to give ourselves the care, devotion, attention and love that we so readily give others. We often console other people when they are down and give them encouraging words when they are insecure, but we are so harsh to our selves. We pick at ourselves and always put ourselves down. When we don't achieve our goals, we are unforgiving to ourselves. Instead of beautifying our natural bodies and features, we seek to change them. What you give to other people, you are the most in need of and the most deserving of it. That is why to love yourself *Fee Sabililah*, is to channel the love back to yourself, as Allah wants you to do. When you take care of your hair and your body, you are loving yourself. When you change your thought patters to affirm your strength, beauty and intelligence you are using your mind to *love* yourself *Fee Sabililah*. Many of us wake up in the morning and always pick at our skin or our facial features and lament on why we are not prettier. When we begin loving ourselves, we will look at ourselves differently. We won't think we are beautiful only when we have on makeup, or only when we have clear skin, or only when our hair is done or only when we are wearing expensive clothes. We will see ourselves as beautiful all the time. Everyday. Irrespective of our makeup, hair and clothing. We will notice all the beautiful things about us that we previously overlooked or undermined. We will admire the creation of Allah. We will use our hands to nourish and take care of ourselves. We will allow our hair to be a unique expression of ourselves. And when we love ourselves, we will be able to give to our loved ones in a deeper and more meaningful way.

In light of this, the second part of this book will explore the ways in which we maintain and use our physicality according to the Prophetic traditions. Enhancing and maintaining our physical appearances is conducive to our spiritual growth.

Inner beauty can be compared to a beautiful, clean garment and outer well-being is the embellishment or the perfume on the cloth. Similarly to a clean garment that has been perfumed, our physical appearance is an indication of our inner contentment. While we explore these beauty techniques, we should remember that these are to be taken in conjunction with inner beauty practices.

Hygiene

"Purity is half of faith." – Prophet of God. (Muslim)

In Islam there is an emphasis on maintaining both spiritual and physical cleanliness. In order to perform many Islamic rituals, we need to be in a state of physical purity. For example, to pray we must make wudu and if we are in a physical state of major impurity, we perform ghusul. This emphasis on cleanliness also extends to maintaining our physical hygiene.

"And Allah loves those who purify themselves" – Quran 9:108

Good physical hygiene translates into positive body image and high self-esteem. When we feel good spiritually, we will develop healthy habits that maintain our bodies, as they are gifts from God. Maintaining cleanliness also ensures that we are conscious of our health and actively seek to safe guard ourselves from contracting infections and diseases. This is not to say that we can always prevent sickness, but by implementing hygienic practices into our lives we can *InshaAllah* maximize the utility of our bodies. This Prophetic tradition ensures that we do not neglect our physical bodies while focusing on the spiritual. To take care of our hair, our nails and teeth is worship. Moreover, it enhances our physical beauty in a healthy manner because it rests on the bedrock of wellbeing.

There is no beauty in self-harm.

In the Quran, Allah stresses the power of knowledge and the arresting effect of ignorance. Learning about how our choices affect the ways in which our bodies function and respond to physical maintenance is empowering. Essentially, we can practice beauty by observing a healthy lifestyle and taking care of ourselves. By looking our best, we will feel better, thus be more enthusiastic in our worship towards Allah. It is lastly important to remember that we are caretakers of our bodies as we were created by God and we will return to Him. Our body parts will speak on the Day of Judgment and inform Allah how we used them. However, our bodies do not wait until Judgment Day to talk to us, because they react to our present self-treatment. When we exercise, we see the effects on our bodies and when we smoke, we also see the effects on our bodies.

So let us properly care and utilize our bodies in ways that when they speak during this life and the next, they will affirm the goodness and love that we showed ourselves.

Nails

There is a practice to grow the nails and paint them with varying colours. We grow our nails because we have been conditioned to view it as elegant however the Prophet highlighted that beauty is in shortening the nails. As appealing as they may appear, longer nails are problematic when we are performing certain tasks and we are more prone to scratch others and ourselves. Moreover, longer nails are more likely to break and therefore we put ourselves in harms way to experience pain. Also many women cannot use the full extent of their hands because of their long nails. We choose to handicap ourselves to maintain beauty standards that were not even constructed by us.

Allah states in the Quran: *"Allah intends for you ease and does not intend for you hardship.." – Quran 2:185*

We should follow the Prophetic traditions in nail practices because it is more convenient, short nails look more professional and they are beneficial for us for hygienic reasons. Therefore instead of looking at the constant changing trends in society, let us focus on the merits of the *Sunan al Fitra.*

Underarm Hair Removal

It is a commonly held myth that this practice is restricted for only women. However this is recommended for both women and men to maintain cleanliness. Many women are growing out their underarm hair in protest against what they perceive to be oppressive gender obligations. While we have an excessive preoccupation in competing with men in our quest for liberation, we forgo implementing the Islamic narratives of beauty.

The most noble human that walked this planet was the Prophet and he prescribed this practice for *both* genders, therefore why do we view this practice as restrictive and oppressive? Removing the hair from the under arms is important because it helps with odor and it improves the appearance of our bodies. Moreover, it gets us in the regular habit of self-care when it comes to taking care of our bodies. Remember our organs such as our sight, heart, livers, kidneys work because Allah causes them to function properly, therefore we must equally take care of our outside appearances to demonstrate our gratitude for our health. Belief involves conviction of the validity of the Quran and the Message that was brought with the Prophet. Faith is the surrender to the guidance that comes as result of this belief however it manifests itself in your life and even if the guidance involves practices that conflict with conventional understandings of beauty. While belief lies in the heart, faith is a continual exercise of decolonization as we are forced to challenge our tightly held societal dogmas, beliefs and biases. Faith is a practice whereby we seek Allah as our Guide to show us the way He wants *us* to worship *Him*, not how *we* think we should worship Him. On the Day of Judgment, we are told that the believers will have a light that will guide them towards Paradise. We need to ask Allah to illuminate our lives and choices in order to lead us to experience tranquility in this world and the next.

Oral Health

Maintaining oral health is important for both health and aesthetic purposes. Good levels of oral health allow us to smile and enjoy various meals without discomfort or pain. Smiling is the Sunnah of the Prophet and maintaining oral health can help us to practice this Sunnah more frequently in the worship of Allah.

In regards to maintaining his oral health, the Prophet would clean his teeth regularly using a twig called the Siwak that is known for its antibacterial and antifungal properties. In fact the Prophet Muhammad stated "if it would not be difficult for my Ummah, I would order them to use Siwak before every salah." (Bukhari) We can see that the Prophet Muhammad made an effort to ward off bad breath and dental issues because he encouraged us to brush our teeth numerous times in the day illustrating his love for cleanliness and hygiene. All that he was on the *inside* was reflected on what he did for his body on the *outside*. His beauty practices were an extension of his beliefs.

The Prophet Muhammad introduced health practices during a time whereby many people were ignorant of basic hygienic practices. The Prophet took a holistic approach to defining beauty in that he did not disproportionally focus on the inner while neglecting the outer, rather true consciousness of Allah, true worship, true beauty involves all of our attention on every part of our bodies. We care for our hearts, bodies and minds as we care for our hair, teeth, skin and nails.

True beauty is not dismembered; rather it is orchestrated into a harmonic symphony that enhances our beauty in its totality. When you describe beauty, we should note that it is an experience that is felt with all our senses not just our eyes. Someone who is truly beautiful will be beautiful in all ways. Therefore it is not enough that we have a radiant smile, rather that smile is the flower, but the scent of this flower is our words.

The Prophet stated " Whoever believes in Allah and the Last Day, should speak a good word or remain silent." (Bukhari)

Beautiful teeth and beautiful words should go together and not be separated in order to maximize our happiness. What begins in our hearts reflects onto different aspects in our lives. A gardener knows that flowers need fertile soil, daily watering and a sufficient amount of sunlight to grow.

Similarly to be beautiful we need to be consistent in our practices. Take care of your teeth when you are lazy, when you are busy, when you are tired and speak good words when you are lazy, busy and tired. Use your mouth to speak with integrity, purpose, love and truth. We see that the Prophet Muhammad embodied the true meaning of oral health in that his words, his gums, his teeth and tongue were clean and used to produce love and clarity into the world.

Hair

"He who has hair should honour it." – Prophet of God (Abu Dawud)

Hair shapes our identities and influences how we enter spaces with our personal styles. As women, our hair is the accessary to our features as it complements our facial beauty. It is well known that we have been ordered by Allah to cover our hair from non-mahram men. Therefore, our covering adds a spiritual significance to our hair and an exclusivity. In that, unlike many other religions and cultures, there are parameters in who can visually consume our hair. Hair is an extension of our faith. This is not to say that because we wear the veil, that we forgo maintaining and grooming ourselves. In fact we see from the Prophet's statement that because hair is weighty in the spiritual sense it reinforces its aesthetic significance. What is beautiful with God will always be beautiful, however and to whomever it chooses to appear.

Because we can uncover our hair to believing women and our close male family members, this strengthens familial ties, sisterhood and therefore removes layers of barriers among women. This sisterhood bond created through the uncovering of hair silently states that we are close regardless of ethnicity, languages and social status.

To honour our hair means that we should be attentive to it and use the necessary products that will strengthen and nourish our hair. To engage in the acts of self-care is a manifestation of self-love. In that we realize that there is no one who will care for us the way we care for ourselves. We know what is good for our bodies, what hurts and what comforts us. Many women visit the hair salon for hair treatment and hair styling and while this is a disarming and relaxing environment, it is still someone else's hands going through, braiding and massaging our heads. While, one cannot argue that visiting the salon is a form of self care that is sustained through monetary exchange, the act of regular up keep of our hair by our own hands increases our own familiarity with our own hair. It gives us knowledge of our textures, our growth and our colors. Hair is often a realm where we exercise our self-hatred and low self esteem and it is a testament to our distorted understanding of beauty and mental colonization. Instead of letting our hair speak to us, we speak for it. We need to let our bodies introduce themselves to us. They speak in different languages, radiate different hues and grow in different ways. A single hair type does not have monopoly over beauty although we are constantly told that is the case. We often see in magazines and the media that there is an emphasis on straight, flowing hair that incites many women to purchase extensions and chemically altering hair products that change the nature and health of their hair. The Prophet told us to *honour* our hair, therefore let it be a tool of self-definition not one of mimicry or a place of self-assault. Our internal health reflects how we treat our bodies. Many times, we straighten or process our hair for the same reasons we lighten our skin, contour our noses and undergo plastic surgery, to feel beautiful. We seek to be beautiful in the eyes of others, even if it means changing and disregarding the essential aspects of ourselves that add to our uniqueness.

Often times, it is the *same* people, who feel insecure and shameful towards their own hair, that project their insecurities and fears of undesirability on to us by choosing to see beauty through white supremacist lenses. They see beauty as one of conformity, as one of predictability. They seek to make same what Allah made different. It is not our skin tones, our bodies, or our hair that need to be adjusted rather it is their perception.

At the same time, the veil says that you will not be reduced to hair, and you will define beauty in additional ways. You will have to build your self-esteem on something else; not on conforming, not on desirability not on white supremacist ideals. A woman who wears the headscarf is essentially coerced into looking inwards for affirmation and self-acceptance because she is not complimented on her physical beauty to the same extent she would be if she uncovered herself. By wearing the veil, she is shown that no one will ever be enough to societal shifting beauty expectations; therefore self-love and validation must come from somewhere else. It must be built on a different foundation. Hair and the Hijab are intertwined, both inner statements because how you choose to wear and groom your hair and your choice to wear the veil are indications of your inner beliefs and convictions. The veil is a public and inner statement that says that beauty is the marriage between body and soul regardless of the changing narratives. Therefore beauty does not exclusively belong to the youthful, the healthy, the thin and fair, rather beauty is living in all of us and stubbornly persists throughout our lives. You cannot commodify beauty, your spirit and vibrancy cannot be commercialized.

Your body is the kingdom of *you* where you are to exercise inner beauty and self-love.

The Prophet once said that "Allah (swt) is Beautiful and He(swt) loves Beauty" so be beautiful. But be beautiful *to* yourself and *for* yourself. (Muslim)

Eyes

Our eyes are our personal camera lenses through which we view the world and navigate through life. Our eyes serve many functions that allow us to function easier as human beings. They express our emotions whether we are happy or sad. Eyes are used to perceive events, people, animals and objects and work holistically with the other senses to comprehend life situations. Allah states that *"It is He Who has produced you and made for you hearing and vision and hearts (intellect): little are you grateful."* – *Quran* 67:23.

Our five senses affect our hearts and our ability to worship Allah. If anything these gifts are tests for us because they do not filter information. Rather we are presented with ideas, beliefs, opinions, taste and sights that we are to then process in our minds and hearts. We see ugliness and beauty, and we can choose to identify *what* is beautiful or ugly. The interlocutor between our spirit and senses is our minds. How we *perceive* what we see, is a reflection of our inner wellness or lack thereof.

We should strive to take care our eyes by eating wholesome and healthy foods and try avoiding eye harming activities such as watching too much television or using the computer excessively and needlessly.

Moreover, we should not use our eyes to harm others, by inflicting them with the evil within our hearts, superimposing our opinions on them and refusing to see from their standpoint. Our eyes are to be used in conjunction with our minds and hearts for empathy, clarity and fortitude. They are to be used for noticing patterns, behaviors and trends and to evaluate whether things maximize or decrease our health and happiness.

The heart and eyes are connected in this matter, because when we think negatively, *how* we see *what* we see will only reinforce this negativity.

At the start each day, we need to use our eyesight to look for, recognize and create beauty in our lives instead of waiting to be bestowed with it by the kindness of others. Everyday, we are bombarded with negative whispers from the shaytan, whispers of doubt, pain and anxiety that keep us paralyzed. When Allah states that indeed the soul is inclined to evil (Quran 12:53), then when we have the audacity to chase light and beauty instead of ugliness and darkness, we are radical in our celebration of self-love.

To use our eyes in a libratory manner, requires a shift in perception.

"How amazing is the affair of the believer. There is good for him in everything and that is for no one but the believer. If good times come his way, he expresses gratitude to Allah and that is good for him, and if hardship comes his way, he endures it patiently and that is better for him." –The Prophet of God (Muslim)

The believer understands that all seemingly beneficial and harmful things are only an opportunity to grow. If we look at wealth, health and beauty as tests, these ideals will not oppress us. And if we take sickness and poverty to be opportunities of growth, we will not suffer. Everyone will be thrown tests in life that is not our choice. But how we respond to the trial is ours. So *how* you see *what* you see, is connected to your heart and inner beauty.

"A man passed by Allah's Messenger saw and the Prophet asked (his companions) "What do you say about this (man)?" They replied "If he asks for a lady's hand, he ought to be given her in marriage; and if he intercedes (for someone) his intercessor should be accepted; and if he speaks, he should be listened to." Allah's Messenger kept silent, and then a man from among the poor Muslims passed by, an Allah's Messenger saw asked (them) "What do you say about this man?" They replied, "If he asks for a lady's hand in marriage he does not deserve to be married, and he intercedes (for someone), his intercession should not be accepted; And if he speaks, he should not be listened to.' Allah's Messenger saw said, "This poor man is better than so many of the first as filling the earth." (Bukhari)

In the above narration the Prophet teaches us to change our value systems and how we view people. Our eyes are not just for viewing events, they are also used for shaping our perceptions and value systems. Allah wants us to use our eyes in a revolutionary manner that challenges the conventional societal value systems of elitism, the aesthetics of white supremacy, racism, mindless materialism and conformism. Although we are flooded with definitions and images of what success looks like, the Islamic version of success does not come in one box. You do not have to be a millionaire to be successful. You don't even have to be healthy to be successful. People define success after someone has accumulated various worldly gains. Those who have achieved the stamp of "success" thereafter sit on top and discontinue their self-growth process.

However, success is created everyday as a project of reinvention and rejuvenation. Truly successful people are not complacent or relaxed with what they achieved yesterday in terms of inner beauty, rather they know that today is a new day and a new chance to be as good or better. While advertisements and the media, always direct our attention in looking outward to heighten our self worth, truly successful people look within themselves.

When we are humble to Allah in our prayers, we achieve a satisfaction in our minds knowing that He is in control of everything and success comes from Him.

When we turn away from vain and useless speech we have protected ourselves from cannibalism and we have respected the humanity of others.

When we give zakah, we recognize that our rizq comes from Allah and not from our jobs, spouses or families.

When someone is successful they are successful in their speech and conduct. They do not just squander money and engage in destructive behavior. If we look at the life of the most successful man in this world, the Prophet Muhammad, he was successful in how he slept, how he ate, socialized, how he earned and how he *lived.*

In accordance with conventional beauty standards, we have been conditioned to see beauty as someone who is usually fair, tall, slim, with symmetrical facial features. We hold certain types of beauty as the standard and therefore we have conformist and exclusionist understandings of the term. More often then not, this conception of beauty incites self-disdain and self-dissatisfaction in that people who hold a conformist idea of beauty usually engage in practices that poison and deform their bodies to resemble what they believe to be the standard body type. Historically, we have been made to believe that success, civility, beauty, intelligence and virtue are products of white people, and the more closer we are to emulating Western civilization, the more we are considered to be human. Anything that contradicts this understanding is often misrepresented and considered to be repressive and barbaric. This conditioning has been reinforced through religious ideologies that have been misused to justify slavery, colonialism and institutionalized racism. We can look at the Christian depiction of Jesus and how the belief that the Prophet Jesus was god was used to reinforce White supremacist ideas of beauty. When a "redeemed soul" was constantly exposed to this image and made to believe God is white, then subconsciously the differences in living standards, the unequal treatment of people of colour, the exploitation of various countries by Western states became accepted and mistaken for Divine Order.

If the highest virtuous being looks like a white person, then that must mean that they are entitled to the best living standards even if it is at the expense of people of colour. If God is white, then the closer one gets to emulating White supremacist understandings of beauty, class and intelligence, means that she can attain scraps of "virtue" for herself through mimicry and self hate. If God is a white man, then that means that Satan is not white and anything that is associated with blackness is satanic and evil.

On what foundation can you start to build an identity that affirms your humanity, when the very representation of the being you take for a deity is presented in the image that is used to defend the wealth, power and privilege of one group of people over the other?

Images are a powerful tool that can distort our understandings of ourselves in relation to the world. We were created to wrestle with the existential question of what it means to be human and use our minds as a liberating force to affirm the equality and life of all humans.

Allah states about Himself; that *"Nor is there to Him any equivalent" – Quran 112:4*

He is unlike any of His creation, His Beauty, His Grace, His Mercy are unique to Him. Therefore if He is unique, that means that there is no group of people who are closer to or further away from Him by virtue of their skin colour. Black or White. When we understand that, then we see that no one has a monopoly over beauty and it is available to everyone.

You are not beautiful solely due to your whiteness and you are not beautiful only *because* you are black. You are beautiful in your being, in your wholeness, your humanness. Beauty is not limited to the physical form rather it is an experience that encapsulates the person in their fullness.

And He states to humanity:

"O mankind, indeed, We have created you from male and female and made you peoples and tribes that you may know one another. Indeed, the most noble of you in the sight of Allah is the most righteous of you. Indeed, Allah is Knowing and Acquainted." – Quran 49:13

It is through knowledge that we experience the endless amount of ways beauty is manifested. Why try to contain something that was created universal? If the never ending galaxy, the Milky Way and the planets in all their splendor and differences are beautiful, why should we limit beauty to one category, one type and one look?

The beauty that we are looking to heighten depends on the extent in which we exercise self-love and the production of beauty. The Prophet (peace be upon him) stated that:

"Verily, Allah does not look at your appearance or wealth, but rather he looks at your hearts and actions." (Muslim)

One of Allah's Attributes is that He is Beautiful. It is interesting to note that people who are physically beautiful, usually put a great deal of emphasis on the outer appearance of themselves and others. Some even go as far as to base the social stratification of humans on the basis of their looks. However, Allah is the most beautiful in the Truest sense

"His is a veil of light. If He were to remove it, the glory of His countenance would ignite everything of Creation as He looks upon it" (Muslim)

Even with this immense Beauty, Allah places value over the inner beauty of a person over their appearance. If a model were to gush over your beauty, you would feel a rise in your self-esteem and you would believe her affirmations of your physical appearance. But what if the Most Beautiful, said to you that you are beautiful in your own skin. What if the Most Beautiful said to you, you are beautiful when you are content with Allah's Provisions, when you take care of your self, when you value yourself, when you lift others, when you help your community and family. You are beautiful in your worship and embodiment of the Divine Commands in your life. You are beautiful because beauty cannot emanate from anything other than a healthy source.

Inner beauty is cultivated through your choices and actions. When exercising self-love, it is important to be mindful of the harmful images and beliefs that damage our self-esteem.

Allah wants us to turn away from opportunistic harmful images that distort and limit our visions of beauty.

When we turn away from these images, we must find images that speak to us, images that we create and celebrate. Let us look at our mothers, grandmothers, aunts, daughters and friends who work, sacrifice and support those around them. Let us look to the elders in our communities who despite their white hair and wrinkles challenge the belief that beauty is only for the young and continuously inspire us with their wisdom and strength.

These are the kinds of images that we have to internalize and look up to as paradigms of self-actualization and joy.

It is in Islam where we find our affirmation and our strength. It is in that space with our relationship with the All Mighty, where we are given the stamp of approval for our physical appearances. Self-actualization and self-love are awakened in the heart and mind and it is embodied in our choices and actions. When we look at harmful images and in turn perpetuate them though mimicry, we are dishonest with ourselves and others. As Muslim women, we have seen the true images of beauty in our history, communities and our families therefore we need to be harbingers of this understanding. It is through seeing ourselves authentically, that we can end the practice of looking for ourselves in dirty mirrors. We can begin to look through new eyes, enriched with healthy hearts, minds and moist with the drops of wudu on our eyelashes. So how must we **be** beautiful? By simply being for Allah as He created you to be. Loving yourself, honoring yourself and celebrating yourself as a tool to generate beauty onwards and outwards.

Acknowledgments

This work has relied on the Glorious Quran, Saheeh International Translation Published by Maktabah Booksellers and Publishers and the aHadith collections of Sahih Al Bukhari compiled by Imam Muhammad ibn Ismail Al-Bukhari Translated by Dr. Muhammad Muhsin Khan. Darrussalam Publications, Sahih Muslim, compiled by Imam Abdul Hussein Muslim bin Al Hajaj. Translated by Nasiruddin al-Khattab Darussalam Publications, Jami At-Tirmidhi compiled by Imam Hafiz Abu Eisa Mohammed ibn Eisa At-Tirmidhi, Translated by Abu Khallyl Darussalam Publications and Sunan Abu Dawud compiled by Imam Hafiz Abu Dawud Sulaiman bin Ash'ath Translated by Nasiruddin Al Khattab Darussalam Publications.

CPSIA information can be obtained
at www.ICGtesting.com
Printed in the USA
LVHW050044230122
709136LV00010B/842